50 Taste of Mexico Dishes

By: Kelly Johnson

Table of Contents

- Tacos al Pastor
- Enchiladas
- Guacamole
- Tamales
- Mole Poblano
- Chiles Rellenos
- Quesadillas
- Chilaquiles
- Pozole
- Sopes
- Tacos de Carnitas
- Ceviche
- Baja Fish Tacos
- Elote
- Fajitas
- Arroz Rojo
- Frijoles Charros
- Tostadas
- Huevos Rancheros
- Pibil
- Carne Asada
- Alambres
- Salsas de Molcajete
- Pambazos
- Cochinita Pibil
- Caldo de Res
- Gorditas
- Rajas Poblanas
- Empanadas
- Churros
- Bistec a la Mexicana
- Queso Fundido
- Tlacoyos
- Tacos de Barbacoa
- Torta Ahogada

- Pollo en Salsa Verde
- Tacos de Asada
- Menudo
- Aguas Frescas
- Nopales en Salsa
- Tamal de Elote
- Molletes
- Chiles en Nogada
- Pan de Elote
- Tacos de Pescado
- Relleno Negro
- Pipián
- Arroz con Leche
- Manteca de Cerdo
- Flan Mexicano

Tacos al Pastor

Ingredients:

- 1 lb pork shoulder (thinly sliced)
- 1/4 cup pineapple (grated or finely chopped)
- 1/4 cup pineapple juice
- 3 cloves garlic (minced)
- 2 tablespoons achiote paste
- 1 tablespoon chili powder
- 1 tablespoon vinegar
- 1 teaspoon cumin
- 1 teaspoon oregano
- Salt and pepper to taste
- 12 small corn tortillas
- 1/2 cup diced onions
- 1/2 cup chopped cilantro
- Lime wedges for serving

Instructions:

1. **Marinate Pork:** In a bowl, combine pineapple, pineapple juice, garlic, achiote paste, chili powder, vinegar, cumin, oregano, salt, and pepper. Add the sliced pork and marinate for at least 2 hours or overnight.
2. **Cook Pork:** Heat a skillet or grill over medium heat. Cook the marinated pork for 4-5 minutes on each side, until browned and cooked through.
3. **Assemble Tacos:** Warm the tortillas and fill them with the cooked pork. Top with onions, cilantro, and a squeeze of lime.
4. **Serve:** Serve the tacos hot with additional lime wedges.

Enchiladas

Ingredients:

- 12 corn tortillas
- 2 cups cooked chicken (shredded)
- 2 cups red enchilada sauce
- 1 cup shredded cheese (cheddar or Mexican blend)
- 1/2 cup chopped onions
- 1/4 cup chopped cilantro
- 1 tablespoon vegetable oil (for frying tortillas)

Instructions:

1. **Fry Tortillas:** Heat the oil in a pan. Lightly fry each tortilla until soft, about 1-2 minutes on each side. Drain on paper towels.
2. **Assemble Enchiladas:** Preheat the oven to 350°F (175°C). Spread a small amount of enchilada sauce in the bottom of a baking dish. Roll the tortillas with shredded chicken and place them seam-side down in the dish.
3. **Top with Sauce and Cheese:** Pour the remaining enchilada sauce over the rolled tortillas and sprinkle with cheese and chopped onions.
4. **Bake:** Bake for 20-25 minutes, or until the cheese is melted and bubbly.
5. **Serve:** Garnish with cilantro and serve hot.

Guacamole

Ingredients:

- 3 ripe avocados (peeled and mashed)
- 1/2 cup diced tomatoes
- 1/4 cup diced onions
- 1 clove garlic (minced)
- 1 lime (juiced)
- Salt and pepper to taste
- 1/4 cup chopped cilantro

Instructions:

1. **Mash Avocados:** In a bowl, mash the avocados with a fork until smooth but slightly chunky.
2. **Mix Ingredients:** Add tomatoes, onions, garlic, lime juice, cilantro, salt, and pepper. Stir until well combined.
3. **Serve:** Serve immediately with tortilla chips or as a topping for tacos.

Tamales

Ingredients:

- 2 cups masa harina
- 1 cup chicken or vegetable broth
- 1/2 cup vegetable oil
- 1 teaspoon baking powder
- 1 teaspoon salt
- 1 1/2 cups filling (shredded beef, chicken, cheese, or vegetables)
- Corn husks (soaked in warm water)

Instructions:

1. **Prepare Masa:** In a bowl, combine masa harina, baking powder, salt, vegetable oil, and broth. Mix until smooth and pliable.
2. **Assemble Tamales:** Take a soaked corn husk, spread a small amount of masa dough on it, and add a tablespoon of filling. Fold the sides of the husk in and roll it up.
3. **Steam Tamales:** Arrange the tamales upright in a large pot or steamer. Steam for about 1 to 1.5 hours, or until the masa is cooked through.
4. **Serve:** Let the tamales cool slightly before serving.

Mole Poblano

Ingredients:

- 4 dried ancho chilies
- 2 dried pasilla chilies
- 2 dried mulato chilies
- 1/4 cup sesame seeds
- 1/4 cup pumpkin seeds
- 1/4 cup almonds
- 1/4 cup raisins
- 1 tablespoon cumin
- 1 tablespoon cinnamon
- 1/2 teaspoon cloves
- 1/4 cup cocoa powder
- 1/2 cup chicken broth
- 2 tablespoons vegetable oil
- 2 chicken breasts (cooked and shredded)
- 1 onion (chopped)
- 2 cloves garlic (minced)
- 1/2 cup tomato paste
- 1 tablespoon sugar
- Salt to taste

Instructions:

1. **Toast Seeds and Chilies:** In a dry skillet, toast the seeds, chilies, and almonds until fragrant. Remove from heat and let cool.
2. **Blend Sauce:** In a blender, combine the toasted ingredients with cocoa powder, raisins, cumin, cinnamon, cloves, and chicken broth. Blend until smooth.
3. **Cook Mole:** In a large pan, heat oil and sauté onion and garlic until softened. Add the mole sauce and simmer for 15-20 minutes.
4. **Add Chicken:** Stir in the shredded chicken and simmer for an additional 5 minutes.
5. **Serve:** Serve the mole over rice or as a topping for tacos or tamales.

Chiles Rellenos

Ingredients:

- 6 poblano peppers (roasted and peeled)
- 1/2 cup cheese (cheddar or Oaxaca)
- 2 eggs (beaten)
- 1/4 cup flour
- 1/4 cup vegetable oil
- 1/2 cup tomato sauce
- 1/4 cup chopped onions

Instructions:

1. **Prepare Peppers:** Roast the poblano peppers over an open flame or in the oven until the skins are charred. Peel off the skins and remove seeds.
2. **Stuff Peppers:** Stuff each pepper with cheese and secure with toothpicks.
3. **Batter:** Dredge the stuffed peppers in flour, then dip in beaten eggs.
4. **Fry:** Heat oil in a pan and fry the peppers until golden brown on all sides.
5. **Serve:** In a separate pan, sauté onions and add tomato sauce to heat. Serve the peppers topped with the sauce.

Quesadillas

Ingredients:

- 8 flour tortillas
- 2 cups cheese (cheddar, Oaxaca, or a blend)
- 1/2 cup cooked chicken, beef, or vegetables (optional)
- 2 tablespoons vegetable oil

Instructions:

1. **Assemble Quesadillas:** Place cheese (and any additional fillings) between two tortillas.
2. **Cook:** Heat oil in a pan over medium heat. Cook each quesadilla for 2-3 minutes per side, or until golden and cheese is melted.
3. **Serve:** Serve with guacamole, sour cream, or salsa.

Chilaquiles

Ingredients:

- 4 cups tortilla chips
- 2 cups green or red salsa
- 1/2 cup cheese (crumbled cotija or shredded cheddar)
- 2 eggs (fried)
- 1/4 cup chopped onions
- 1/4 cup chopped cilantro
- 1/2 cup sour cream

Instructions:

1. **Cook Salsa:** Heat salsa in a pan over medium heat. Add tortilla chips and stir to coat in the salsa.
2. **Fry Eggs:** In a separate pan, fry the eggs sunny-side up.
3. **Assemble Chilaquiles:** Place the salsa-coated chips on a plate. Top with fried eggs, cheese, onions, cilantro, and sour cream.
4. **Serve:** Serve immediately.

Pozole

Ingredients:

- 2 lbs pork shoulder (cubed)
- 1 onion (chopped)
- 4 cloves garlic (minced)
- 2 cans hominy (drained)
- 2 dried ancho chilies
- 1 tablespoon oregano
- 1 teaspoon cumin
- 1 teaspoon chili powder
- 8 cups chicken broth
- Salt to taste
- Lime wedges, radishes, and shredded cabbage for garnish

Instructions:

1. **Cook Pork:** In a large pot, sauté onion and garlic until softened. Add pork and cook until browned.
2. **Simmer:** Add hominy, chicken broth, chilies, oregano, cumin, and chili powder. Bring to a boil and then simmer for 1-2 hours.
3. **Blend Chilies:** Blend the ancho chilies with a bit of broth and add back to the pot.
4. **Serve:** Garnish with lime wedges, radishes, and shredded cabbage.

Sopes

Ingredients:

- 2 cups masa harina
- 1 cup warm water
- 1/2 teaspoon salt
- 1 cup refried beans
- 1 cup cooked meat (chicken, beef, or pork)
- 1 cup shredded lettuce
- 1/2 cup salsa
- 1/2 cup cheese (crumbled cotija)
- 1/4 cup sour cream

Instructions:

1. **Make Dough:** Mix masa harina, warm water, and salt to form a dough. Divide into small balls and flatten into thick discs.
2. **Cook Sopes:** Heat a skillet and cook the discs for 2-3 minutes on each side until golden and firm.
3. **Assemble Sopes:** Top each sope with refried beans, cooked meat, lettuce, salsa, cheese, and sour cream.
4. **Serve:** Serve warm.

Tacos de Carnitas

Ingredients:

- 3 lbs pork shoulder (cut into chunks)
- 1 onion (quartered)
- 4 cloves garlic (minced)
- 2 oranges (juiced)
- 2 tablespoons lime juice
- 1 tablespoon cumin
- 1 tablespoon oregano
- 1 tablespoon chili powder
- 1 bay leaf
- Salt and pepper to taste
- 12 small corn tortillas
- 1/2 cup chopped onions
- 1/2 cup cilantro
- Lime wedges for serving

Instructions:

1. **Cook the Pork:** In a large pot, add pork, onion, garlic, orange juice, lime juice, cumin, oregano, chili powder, bay leaf, salt, and pepper. Add enough water to cover the meat. Bring to a boil, then reduce the heat to a simmer and cook for about 2 hours or until the pork is tender and easy to shred.
2. **Shred the Pork:** Remove the pork from the pot and shred it using two forks.
3. **Crisp the Pork:** Heat a skillet over medium-high heat, and cook the shredded pork in batches, pressing it down until it becomes crispy on the edges.
4. **Assemble Tacos:** Warm the tortillas and fill them with the crispy carnitas. Top with chopped onions, cilantro, and a squeeze of lime.
5. **Serve:** Serve the tacos with extra lime wedges.

Ceviche

Ingredients:

- 1 lb fresh fish or shrimp (diced)
- 1 cup fresh lime juice
- 1/2 cup diced red onion
- 1 tomato (diced)
- 1 cucumber (peeled and diced)
- 1 avocado (diced)
- 1/4 cup cilantro (chopped)
- 1 serrano pepper (finely chopped)
- Salt and pepper to taste

Instructions:

1. **Marinate Fish or Shrimp:** In a bowl, combine the fish or shrimp with lime juice. Let it sit for at least 30 minutes, or until the fish is opaque and fully "cooked" by the acid.
2. **Prepare Vegetables:** In a separate bowl, mix the onion, tomato, cucumber, avocado, cilantro, and serrano pepper.
3. **Combine:** Once the fish or shrimp is ready, mix it with the vegetables and season with salt and pepper.
4. **Serve:** Serve chilled, garnished with extra cilantro or lime wedges.

Baja Fish Tacos

Ingredients:

- 1 lb white fish fillets (like cod or tilapia)
- 1 cup flour
- 1 teaspoon paprika
- 1 teaspoon cumin
- 1/2 teaspoon chili powder
- Salt and pepper to taste
- 1 cup beer (or sparkling water)
- 2 tablespoons cornstarch
- 1 tablespoon lime juice
- 12 small corn tortillas
- 1/2 cup cabbage (shredded)
- 1/4 cup cilantro (chopped)
- 1/4 cup crema or sour cream
- Salsa for serving

Instructions:

1. **Prepare the Batter:** In a bowl, combine flour, paprika, cumin, chili powder, salt, and pepper. Add the beer (or sparkling water) and cornstarch, and whisk until smooth.
2. **Cook the Fish:** Heat oil in a skillet over medium heat. Dip the fish fillets in the batter and fry until golden brown and cooked through, about 4 minutes per side.
3. **Assemble Tacos:** Warm the tortillas and place a piece of fish on each. Top with shredded cabbage, cilantro, and a drizzle of crema or sour cream.
4. **Serve:** Serve with salsa and extra lime wedges.

Elote (Mexican Street Corn)

Ingredients:

- 4 ears of corn (shucked)
- 1/4 cup mayonnaise
- 1/4 cup crema
- 1 tablespoon chili powder
- 1/2 cup crumbled cotija cheese
- Lime wedges for serving

Instructions:

1. **Grill the Corn:** Grill the corn over medium heat, turning every 2-3 minutes, until lightly charred (about 10 minutes).
2. **Prepare the Topping:** In a bowl, mix the mayonnaise, crema, and chili powder.
3. **Coat the Corn:** Once the corn is grilled, brush it with the mayo-crema mixture and sprinkle with cotija cheese.
4. **Serve:** Serve with lime wedges for squeezing.

Fajitas

Ingredients:

- 1 lb flank steak or chicken breast (sliced thin)
- 1 onion (sliced)
- 1 bell pepper (sliced)
- 2 tablespoons vegetable oil
- 1 tablespoon lime juice
- 1 teaspoon cumin
- 1 teaspoon chili powder
- Salt and pepper to taste
- 8 flour tortillas
- Sour cream, guacamole, and salsa for serving

Instructions:

1. **Marinate the Meat:** In a bowl, combine the meat with lime juice, cumin, chili powder, salt, and pepper. Let it marinate for at least 30 minutes.
2. **Cook the Vegetables:** In a skillet, heat oil over medium heat. Add the onion and bell pepper and sauté until soft, about 5-7 minutes. Remove and set aside.
3. **Cook the Meat:** In the same skillet, cook the marinated meat until browned and cooked through, about 4-5 minutes.
4. **Serve:** Serve the fajitas with warm tortillas, sautéed vegetables, and your choice of toppings like sour cream, guacamole, and salsa.

Arroz Rojo (Mexican Red Rice)

Ingredients:

- 1 cup long-grain white rice
- 2 tablespoons vegetable oil
- 1/2 cup tomato sauce
- 1 1/2 cups chicken broth
- 1/2 cup chopped onions
- 1/2 cup peas
- 1/2 teaspoon cumin
- Salt and pepper to taste

Instructions:

1. **Cook Rice:** Heat oil in a skillet over medium heat. Add rice and cook, stirring constantly, until lightly browned.
2. **Add Ingredients:** Add onions and cook until soft, about 3 minutes. Stir in the tomato sauce, chicken broth, cumin, salt, and pepper.
3. **Simmer:** Bring to a boil, then reduce heat to low. Cover and simmer for 15-20 minutes, until the rice is tender and the liquid is absorbed.
4. **Serve:** Fluff the rice with a fork and serve with peas sprinkled on top.

Frijoles Charros (Mexican Charro Beans)

Ingredients:

- 2 cups pinto beans (soaked overnight)
- 6 cups water or chicken broth
- 1/2 lb bacon (chopped)
- 1 onion (chopped)
- 3 cloves garlic (minced)
- 1 jalapeño (sliced)
- 2 tomatoes (chopped)
- 1/2 teaspoon cumin
- Salt and pepper to taste
- 1/2 cup cilantro (chopped)

Instructions:

1. **Cook the Beans:** In a large pot, add the soaked beans and water (or broth). Bring to a boil, then reduce to a simmer for 1-2 hours, until the beans are tender.
2. **Cook the Bacon:** In a separate pan, cook bacon until crispy. Remove and set aside.
3. **Sauté Vegetables:** In the same pan, sauté onion, garlic, and jalapeño until soft. Add tomatoes and cook for 5 minutes.
4. **Combine:** Add the sautéed vegetables, bacon, cumin, salt, and pepper to the beans. Simmer for an additional 10 minutes.
5. **Serve:** Garnish with chopped cilantro and serve.

Tostadas

Ingredients:

- 10 tostada shells (store-bought or homemade)
- 1 can refried beans (or black beans)
- 1 cup cooked chicken, beef, or shrimp
- 1 cup lettuce (shredded)
- 1/2 cup tomatoes (chopped)
- 1/4 cup cheese (shredded)
- 1/4 cup sour cream
- Salsa for serving

Instructions:

1. **Assemble Tostadas:** Spread a layer of refried beans on each tostada shell. Top with meat, lettuce, tomatoes, and cheese.
2. **Serve:** Add sour cream and salsa on top before serving.

Huevos Rancheros

Ingredients:

- 4 eggs
- 2 corn tortillas
- 1/2 cup ranchero sauce (store-bought or homemade)
- 1/4 cup cheese (crumbled cotija or shredded cheddar)
- 1/4 cup cilantro (chopped)
- 1/4 cup sour cream
- Lime wedges for serving

Instructions:

1. **Fry Tortillas:** Heat oil in a pan and fry the tortillas until crispy but still soft in the center. Remove and set aside.
2. **Cook Eggs:** In the same pan, fry the eggs sunny-side up.
3. **Assemble Huevos Rancheros:** Place a fried tortilla on each plate, top with a fried egg, and pour ranchero sauce over it. Sprinkle with cheese and cilantro.
4. **Serve:** Serve with sour cream and lime wedges.

Pibil

Ingredients:

- 3 lbs pork shoulder (cut into chunks)
- 1/4 cup achiote paste
- 1/2 cup orange juice
- 1/4 cup lime juice
- 3 cloves garlic (minced)
- 1 teaspoon cumin
- 1 teaspoon oregano
- 1/2 cup banana leaves (optional)
- Salt and pepper to taste
- 1/2 cup pickled red onions (for garnish)

Instructions:

1. **Marinate the Meat:** In a bowl, mix achiote paste, orange juice, lime juice, garlic, cumin, oregano, salt, and pepper. Coat the pork with this marinade and refrigerate for at least 4 hours, preferably overnight.
2. **Wrap and Cook:** If using banana leaves, soften them by heating them over a flame. Wrap the marinated pork in the banana leaves (or just use foil). Place in a baking dish and bake at 350°F (175°C) for 2-3 hours or until tender.
3. **Serve:** Shred the pork and serve with pickled red onions.

Carne Asada

Ingredients:

- 2 lbs flank steak or skirt steak
- 1/4 cup lime juice
- 2 tablespoons orange juice
- 3 cloves garlic (minced)
- 1 tablespoon cumin
- 1 tablespoon chili powder
- 1/2 teaspoon cayenne pepper
- 1/4 cup cilantro (chopped)
- Salt and pepper to taste
- 12 tortillas for serving

Instructions:

1. **Marinate the Steak:** Combine lime juice, orange juice, garlic, cumin, chili powder, cayenne, cilantro, salt, and pepper in a bowl. Place the steak in a resealable bag or shallow dish and pour marinade over it. Refrigerate for at least 1 hour.
2. **Cook the Steak:** Heat a grill or skillet over high heat. Grill the steak for about 5-7 minutes per side, or until desired doneness.
3. **Serve:** Slice the steak thinly and serve with tortillas.

Alambres

Ingredients:

- 1 lb skirt steak or chicken breast (cut into cubes)
- 1 onion (sliced)
- 1 bell pepper (sliced)
- 1/2 cup bacon (chopped)
- 1/2 cup cheese (Mexican melting cheese, such as Oaxaca or Monterrey Jack)
- 2 tablespoons vegetable oil
- 1 teaspoon cumin
- Salt and pepper to taste
- Tortillas for serving

Instructions:

1. **Cook the Bacon:** In a large skillet, cook the bacon over medium heat until crispy. Remove and set aside.
2. **Cook the Meat:** In the same skillet, heat the oil and cook the cubed steak or chicken until browned and cooked through.
3. **Add Vegetables:** Add the onions and bell pepper to the pan and sauté until softened.
4. **Combine:** Stir in the cooked bacon, cumin, salt, and pepper. Sprinkle the cheese over the top and cover the skillet until the cheese melts.
5. **Serve:** Serve the alambres with warm tortillas.

Salsas de Molcajete

Ingredients:

- 2 tomatoes (roasted)
- 1/4 onion (roasted)
- 1 jalapeño (roasted)
- 2 cloves garlic (roasted)
- 1/4 cup cilantro (chopped)
- Salt to taste

Instructions:

1. **Roast the Vegetables:** Place the tomatoes, onion, jalapeño, and garlic on a skillet over medium heat. Roast until charred on all sides.
2. **Grind the Salsa:** In a molcajete or mortar and pestle, combine the roasted vegetables and grind until smooth. Add cilantro and salt to taste.
3. **Serve:** Serve the salsa with chips or as a topping for tacos.

Pambazos

Ingredients:

- 6 bolillo rolls (or Mexican sandwich rolls)
- 2 cups potato (peeled and diced)
- 1/2 cup chorizo (cooked)
- 1/2 cup lettuce (shredded)
- 1/2 cup salsa roja
- 1 tablespoon vegetable oil

Instructions:

1. **Prepare the Potato Filling:** Boil the potatoes until tender, then mash them. Mix in the cooked chorizo.
2. **Prepare the Pambazos:** Heat oil in a skillet. Slice the bolillo rolls in half and dip them quickly into the salsa roja, then fry them in the skillet until crispy on both sides.
3. **Assemble:** Spread the potato and chorizo filling on the rolls and top with lettuce.
4. **Serve:** Serve the pambazos immediately, while crispy.

Cochinita Pibil

Ingredients:

- 3 lbs pork shoulder (cut into chunks)
- 1/4 cup achiote paste
- 1/2 cup orange juice
- 1/4 cup lime juice
- 3 cloves garlic (minced)
- 1 teaspoon cumin
- 1 teaspoon oregano
- 1/2 cup banana leaves (optional)
- Salt and pepper to taste
- Pickled red onions (for garnish)

Instructions:

1. **Marinate the Pork:** In a bowl, mix achiote paste, orange juice, lime juice, garlic, cumin, oregano, salt, and pepper. Coat the pork with this marinade and refrigerate for at least 4 hours or overnight.
2. **Wrap and Cook:** Wrap the marinated pork in banana leaves (if using) or foil. Bake at 350°F (175°C) for 3 hours or until the pork is tender and easily shredded.
3. **Serve:** Shred the pork and serve with pickled red onions.

Caldo de Res (Beef Soup)

Ingredients:

- 2 lbs beef shank or bone-in beef short ribs
- 1 onion (quartered)
- 3 cloves garlic (peeled)
- 2 tomatoes (chopped)
- 3 carrots (peeled and chopped)
- 2 potatoes (peeled and chopped)
- 1/2 cup corn kernels
- 1 zucchini (chopped)
- 1/4 cup cilantro (chopped)
- Salt and pepper to taste

Instructions:

1. **Cook the Beef:** In a large pot, add beef and enough water to cover it. Bring to a boil, then reduce heat to a simmer and cook for 2-3 hours until the meat is tender.
2. **Add Vegetables:** Add the onion, garlic, tomatoes, carrots, potatoes, corn, zucchini, and seasoning. Simmer for an additional 30 minutes.
3. **Serve:** Garnish with cilantro and serve with tortillas.

Gorditas

Ingredients:

- 2 cups masa harina
- 1 1/2 cups warm water
- 1 teaspoon baking powder
- 1 teaspoon salt
- Filling of your choice (e.g., cheese, beans, or shredded meat)

Instructions:

1. **Prepare the Dough:** In a bowl, mix masa harina, baking powder, and salt. Gradually add water and knead until a smooth dough forms.
2. **Form the Gorditas:** Divide the dough into small balls. Flatten each ball into a thick disc.
3. **Cook the Gorditas:** Heat a skillet over medium heat. Cook the gorditas for 4-5 minutes on each side, or until golden brown.
4. **Fill the Gorditas:** Slice the gorditas open and fill with your desired fillings.
5. **Serve:** Serve with salsa and sour cream.

Rajas Poblanas

Ingredients:

- 4 poblano peppers (roasted and peeled)
- 1 onion (sliced)
- 1 cup corn kernels
- 1/2 cup heavy cream
- 1/2 cup cheese (Mexican melting cheese)
- Salt and pepper to taste

Instructions:

1. **Prepare the Poblano Peppers:** Roast the poblanos over an open flame until charred. Peel off the skins, remove the seeds, and slice the peppers into strips.
2. **Cook the Vegetables:** In a skillet, sauté the onions and corn until softened. Add the poblano strips and cook for another 5 minutes.
3. **Add Cream and Cheese:** Stir in the heavy cream and cheese. Cook until the cheese is melted and the mixture is creamy.
4. **Serve:** Season with salt and pepper and serve with tortillas.

Empanadas

Ingredients:

- 2 cups all-purpose flour
- 1/2 teaspoon salt
- 1/2 cup butter (cold)
- 1/2 cup water
- 2 cups filling (e.g., sweetened fruit, meat, or cheese)
- 1 egg (beaten)

Instructions:

1. **Prepare the Dough:** In a bowl, combine the flour and salt. Cut in the butter until the mixture resembles coarse crumbs. Gradually add water and knead until the dough forms a ball.
2. **Fill and Seal:** Roll the dough into discs, place a spoonful of filling in the center, and fold over. Press the edges to seal.
3. **Bake:** Brush the empanadas with beaten egg and bake at 350°F (175°C) for 20-25 minutes or until golden brown.
4. **Serve:** Serve warm.

Churros

Ingredients:

- 1 cup water
- 2 tablespoons butter
- 1 tablespoon sugar
- 1/4 teaspoon salt
- 1 cup all-purpose flour
- 1 egg
- 1/2 teaspoon vanilla extract
- Oil for frying
- Cinnamon sugar (for coating)

Instructions:

1. **Make the Dough:** In a saucepan, bring water, butter, sugar, and salt to a boil. Remove from heat and stir in the flour until smooth. Let cool for a few minutes, then beat in the egg and vanilla.
2. **Fry the Churros:** Heat oil in a frying pan to 350°F (175°C). Pipe the dough into the hot oil in strips, frying until golden brown.
3. **Coat and Serve:** Roll the churros in cinnamon sugar and serve with chocolate sauce for dipping.

Bistec a la Mexicana

Ingredients:

- 2 lbs beef steak (cut into small cubes)
- 2 tomatoes (chopped)
- 1 onion (diced)
- 1 jalapeño (sliced)
- 2 cloves garlic (minced)
- 1/2 teaspoon cumin
- 1/2 teaspoon paprika
- 2 tablespoons vegetable oil
- Salt and pepper to taste
- Fresh cilantro (chopped, for garnish)

Instructions:

1. **Cook the Beef:** Heat oil in a skillet over medium-high heat. Add the beef cubes and cook until browned on all sides.
2. **Prepare the Sauce:** In the same skillet, add the onion, garlic, and jalapeño, sautéing until softened.
3. **Add the Tomatoes:** Add the chopped tomatoes, cumin, paprika, salt, and pepper. Stir everything together and cook for 5-7 minutes, until the sauce thickens.
4. **Serve:** Garnish with fresh cilantro and serve with rice or tortillas.

Queso Fundido

Ingredients:

- 2 cups shredded Oaxaca cheese (or other Mexican melting cheese)
- 1/2 cup chorizo (cooked)
- 1/2 cup bell pepper (diced)
- 1/4 cup onion (diced)
- 1 tablespoon vegetable oil
- 1/4 cup fresh cilantro (chopped, for garnish)

Instructions:

1. **Cook the Chorizo:** In a skillet, cook the chorizo over medium heat until fully cooked. Set aside.
2. **Prepare the Queso:** In the same skillet, heat oil and sauté the bell pepper and onion until softened.
3. **Melt the Cheese:** Add the shredded cheese and chorizo to the skillet, stirring until the cheese is melted and gooey.
4. **Serve:** Garnish with cilantro and serve with warm tortillas or tortilla chips.

Tlacoyos

Ingredients:

- 2 cups masa harina
- 1/4 cup cooked black beans (or pinto beans)
- 1/2 teaspoon salt
- 1 cup warm water
- 1/2 cup queso fresco (crumbled)
- 1 tablespoon vegetable oil

Instructions:

1. **Prepare the Dough:** In a bowl, mix masa harina, salt, and warm water. Knead until a smooth dough forms.
2. **Stuff the Tlacoyos:** Take a small portion of dough and flatten it into an oval shape. Place a small amount of beans in the center, then fold the dough over to seal the edges.
3. **Cook the Tlacoyos:** Heat oil in a skillet over medium heat. Cook the tlacoyos for 2-3 minutes on each side until golden brown and crispy.
4. **Serve:** Top with crumbled queso fresco and serve with salsa.

Tacos de Barbacoa

Ingredients:

- 3 lbs beef chuck roast (or lamb, traditional for barbacoa)
- 2 tablespoons chili powder
- 1 teaspoon cumin
- 1/2 teaspoon oregano
- 1/2 onion (quartered)
- 2 cloves garlic (minced)
- 1/4 cup lime juice
- 2 cups beef broth
- Corn tortillas
- Fresh cilantro (for garnish)
- Salsa (optional)

Instructions:

1. **Prepare the Barbacoa:** Rub the beef with chili powder, cumin, oregano, salt, and pepper. Place it in a slow cooker with onion, garlic, lime juice, and beef broth.
2. **Cook the Beef:** Cook on low for 6-8 hours until the beef is tender and easy to shred.
3. **Assemble the Tacos:** Shred the beef and serve in warm tortillas with cilantro and salsa.

Torta Ahogada

Ingredients:

- 2 bolillo rolls (or other crusty Mexican rolls)
- 2 cups carnitas (shredded pork)
- 1 cup salsa de chile de arbol
- 1 onion (sliced)
- 1/2 cup pickled jalapeños
- 1/2 cup avocado (sliced)
- Lime wedges for serving

Instructions:

1. **Prepare the Salsa:** In a blender, blend the dried chiles with garlic, tomatoes, and water to make the salsa de chile de arbol.
2. **Assemble the Torta:** Slice the bolillo rolls and stuff with carnitas, onions, and avocado.
3. **Soak the Torta:** Pour the salsa over the torta until it's soaked through.
4. **Serve:** Serve with lime wedges and pickled jalapeños on the side.

Pollo en Salsa Verde

Ingredients:

- 4 chicken breasts or thighs
- 2 cups tomatillos (husks removed)
- 1/2 onion (diced)
- 2 cloves garlic (minced)
- 1 jalapeño (optional)
- 1/4 cup cilantro (chopped)
- 1 tablespoon vegetable oil
- Salt and pepper to taste

Instructions:

1. **Prepare the Salsa:** In a saucepan, bring the tomatillos, onion, garlic, and jalapeño to a boil in water. Simmer for 10 minutes, then blend until smooth.
2. **Cook the Chicken:** In a skillet, heat oil and cook the chicken until browned on both sides.
3. **Simmer the Chicken:** Pour the salsa verde over the chicken and simmer for 20 minutes until the chicken is fully cooked.
4. **Serve:** Garnish with cilantro and serve with rice or tortillas.

Tacos de Asada

Ingredients:

- 2 lbs flank steak (or skirt steak)
- 1/4 cup lime juice
- 3 cloves garlic (minced)
- 1/4 cup olive oil
- 1 teaspoon cumin
- Salt and pepper to taste
- Corn tortillas
- Fresh cilantro and onion (for garnish)
- Salsa (optional)

Instructions:

1. **Marinate the Steak:** Combine lime juice, garlic, olive oil, cumin, salt, and pepper. Marinate the steak for at least 1 hour.
2. **Grill the Steak:** Heat a grill or skillet to medium-high. Grill the steak for 4-6 minutes per side, or until desired doneness.
3. **Slice and Serve:** Slice the steak thinly and serve in warm tortillas, garnished with cilantro, onion, and salsa.

Menudo

Ingredients:

- 3 lbs beef tripe (cleaned and cut into strips)
- 1 onion (quartered)
- 2 cloves garlic (minced)
- 2 cups beef broth
- 2 dried guajillo chiles (or other dried chiles)
- 2 tablespoons hominy (canned or frozen)
- 1/2 teaspoon oregano
- Salt to taste
- Lime wedges and cilantro (for garnish)

Instructions:

1. **Cook the Tripe:** In a large pot, cook the tripe in water with onion, garlic, and salt for 2-3 hours until tender.
2. **Prepare the Chile Sauce:** Soak the guajillo chiles in hot water for 10 minutes. Blend the softened chiles with a bit of the broth to make a sauce.
3. **Simmer the Soup:** Add the hominy, chile sauce, and oregano to the pot. Simmer for another 30 minutes.
4. **Serve:** Serve with lime wedges and fresh cilantro.

Aguas Frescas

Ingredients:

- 4 cups fresh fruit (e.g., watermelon, pineapple, or hibiscus flowers)
- 4 cups water
- 1/4 cup sugar (adjust to taste)
- 1 tablespoon lime juice

Instructions:

1. **Blend the Fruit:** Blend the fruit with water and sugar until smooth.
2. **Strain:** Strain the mixture through a fine sieve or cheesecloth to remove any pulp.
3. **Serve:** Pour the agua fresca over ice and add a squeeze of lime juice. Serve chilled.

www.ingramcontent.com/pod-product-compliance
Lightning Source LLC
LaVergne TN
LVHW062000070526
838199LV00060B/4208